Bridges

{IT CHANGED THE WORLD}

INVENTION OF
ELECTRICITY

Robin Koontz

Rourke
Educational Media

A Division of
Carson Dellosa Education®

rourkeeducationalmedia.com

BEFORE AND DURING READING ACTIVITIES

Before Reading: *Building Background Knowledge and Vocabulary*

Building background knowledge can help children process new information and build upon what they already know. Before reading a book, it is important to tap into what children already know about the topic. This will help them develop their vocabulary and increase their reading comprehension.

Questions and Activities to Build Background Knowledge:

1. Look at the front cover of the book and read the title. What do you think this book will be about?
2. What do you already know about this topic?
3. Take a book walk and skim the pages. Look at the table of contents, photographs, captions, and bold words. Did these text features give you any information or predictions about what you will read in this book?

Vocabulary: *Vocabulary Is Key to Reading Comprehension*

Use the following directions to prompt a conversation about each word.

- Read the vocabulary words.
- What comes to mind when you see each word?
- What do you think each word means?

Vocabulary Words:

- cinema
- convert
- currents
- electrons
- greenhouse gases
- hydraulic
- incandescent
- innovations
- transmitted
- voltage

During Reading: *Reading for Meaning and Understanding*

To achieve deep comprehension of a book, children are encouraged to use close reading strategies. During reading, it is important to have children stop and make connections. These connections result in deeper analysis and understanding of a book.

Close Reading a Text

During reading, have children stop and talk about the following:

- Any confusing parts
- Any unknown words
- Text to text, text to self, text to world connections
- The main idea in each chapter or heading

Encourage children to use context clues to determine the meaning of any unknown words. These strategies will help children learn to analyze the text more thoroughly as they read.

When you are finished reading this book, turn to the next-to-last page for **Text-Dependent Questions** and an **Extension Activity**.

TABLE OF CONTENTS

LIFE BEFORE ELECTRICITY

Think about all of the things around you right now that use electricity—lights, phones, appliances, and more. Can you imagine life without them? Human civilizations survived without electricity for thousands of years. In the past, people got heat and light from burning animal fat or wax. Later, they used coal, oil, kerosene, or natural gas.

Fire-powered clay ovens or cast-iron stoves were used to cook food and provide heat. Gas-powered stoves were introduced in the early 1800s.

SHELL LAMPS

Some early lamps were just natural containers that held slow-burning material. Moss was often soaked in animal fat, placed inside a shell or a hollow rock, and burned.

The heat in this stove comes from burning wood.

How long do you think your favorite food would last without refrigeration before it went bad? Before electricity, refrigeration was limited, and food spoiled quickly as a result. People stored ice and snow inside an insulated icehouse to keep foods cold year-round. Meat was salted and dried so it could be stored without spoiling.

Ice services such as this one, in business around the 1890s, delivered ice to homes by wagon.

Lots of jobs were different without electricity. People used working animals or **hydraulic** power to grind grain, saw wood, hammer flax for cloth and paper, and crush rocks for roads. They harnessed wind energy using windmills and sails. Later, coal and other fuels were burned to power steam engines.

Wood, fat, oil, natural gas, coal, wind, and water were all used as energy sources before electricity, but they were limited and could be difficult to gather or purchase. Life changed in many ways when electric power was first harnessed.

ELECTRIC PIONEERS

Electricity is the result of the movement of small charged particles called **electrons**. When electrons move, they create electricity. The movement of electricity results in **currents**, which can have different directions. Pioneering scientists in electricity studied this and how some materials conduct, or enable the movement of, electricity.

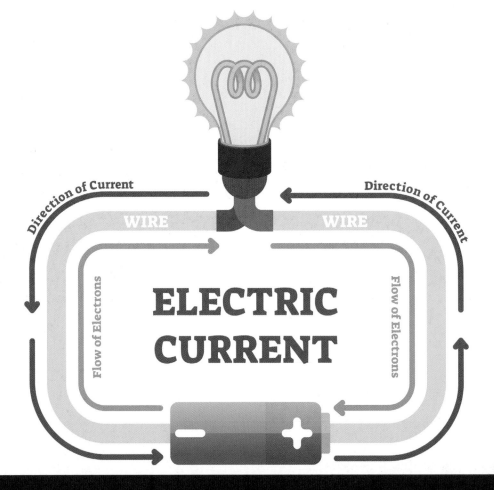

Direction of Current

Direction of Current

WIRE

WIRE

Flow of Electrons

Flow of Electrons

ELECTRIC CURRENT

You might have heard a folktale about Benjamin Franklin's kite being struck by lightning. In 1752, Ben Franklin proved that lightning and electric sparks are the same thing. By 1800, Alessandro Volta had built the first electric battery. It could produce a steady electric current. He also **transmitted** electricity in a controlled way for the first time. **Voltage**, the force that makes electric charges move, is named after him.

SPARKING FUR

Around the year 600 BCE, ancient Greeks experimented by rubbing fur on amber. The fur created sparks of static electricity that could be seen and felt.

Michael Faraday was another electricity pioneer. In 1831, he created a power generator using magnets built on the ideas of Benjamin Franklin and others. Power generators **convert** energy from motion into electrical energy. Electric lights were soon to follow.

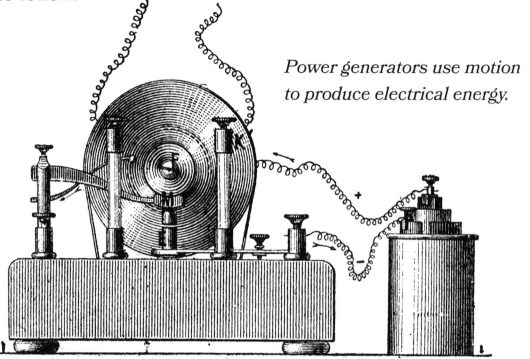

Power generators use motion to produce electrical energy.

AYRTON'S ARC LIGHTS

Hertha Ayrton was the first person to study arc lighting and discover that oxygen caused the lights to hiss and flicker. In 1906, she became the first woman to win a Hughes Medal for her research. Although many scientific societies rejected her membership at the time, her success led to more groups accepting women as members.

The first electric lights were arc lamps in which two pieces of carbon are connected to an electricity supply. Both Thomas Edison and Joseph Swan invented the first filament light bulbs around 1878. Their **incandescent** bulbs could stay lit for many hours. The system used direct current (DC). In a direct current, the current flows in a single direction.

After arc lamps (left) came filament bulbs (center). Bulbs filled with gas (right) replaced incandescent bulbs.

A few years later, Nikola Tesla invented a system that used alternating current (AC), in which the current flows in changing directions. This invention would go on to change how electricity was used.

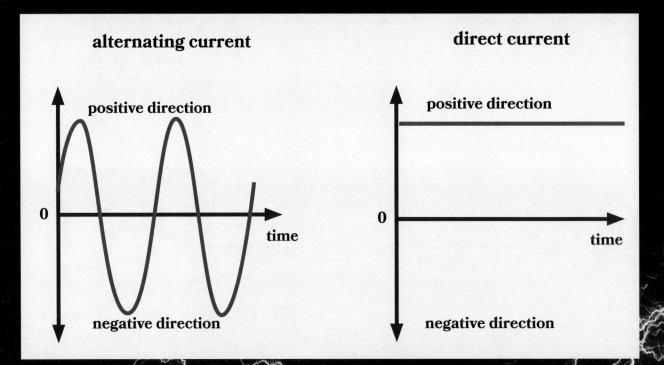

TESLA'S BOATS

Nikola Tesla designed the first remote-controlled boats. When he demonstrated them to the public in 1898, people were amazed. The technology was so incredible that some people thought that magic moved the boats. Others suspected that the boats were driven by trained monkeys.

THE EVOLUTION OF ELECTRICITY

E dison's light bulb was only the beginning of the age
of electricity. It introduced people to a new kind
of energy. Edison and other inventors designed
hundreds of new devices that could run on electricity.

For electricity to be useful to lots of people, it first had to be available to them. Edison opened the first central power generator in 1882 in New York City, Pearl Street Station.

Edison's "jumbo dynamo" was larger than many rooms. Six of these huge machines were used at Pearl Street Station.

If you have ever been to a fair or carnival, you know that they can use a lot of electricity. George Westinghouse provided electrical power for the Chicago World's Fair, a giant event, in 1893. Westinghouse provided AC electricity. This was less expensive than DC electricity.

The Chicago World's Fair was lit by giant lights. This floodlight was 4.9 feet (1.5 meters) across and the largest in the world at the time.

AC power soon became the standard for electricity. Power generators were built on Niagara Falls in the state of New York. Special devices harnessed the energy of the water rushing over the falls and converted it into electricity. By 1902, Niagara Falls was generating one-fifth of the electricity in the United States.

Appliances, power grids, turbine systems, and other electric **innovations** soon came along. The power of electricity had made its mark on the world.

THE WAR OF THE CURRENTS

Edison made a lot of money from the invention of DC power. He tried to discourage the use of AC power, which Telsa helped develop. This rivalry became known as the War of the Currents.

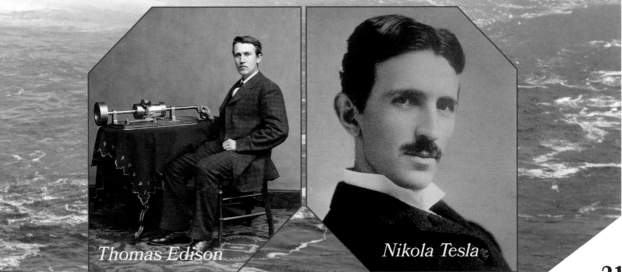

Thomas Edison

Nikola Tesla

CHANGING LIFESTYLES

Electricity changed the way people lived, worked, and spent their free time. Advancements in manufacturing along with electricity made for rapid growth in production, communication, and transportation. Cities grew quickly as a result.

With electricity, builders could construct taller buildings because electric elevators could bring people to the top floors safely and quickly. The addition of electric power made subways and other mass-transit systems faster, safer, and more efficient than transporting a few people at a time. With electrical light available almost everywhere, people could work longer hours.

Early subway cars often had open sides, like these in Brooklyn, New York, around 1910.

Homes began to resemble modern-day households, full of technology powered by electricity. Electric heaters kept people warm, and air conditioning kept them cool. Electric-powered radios—and, later, televisions—provided news, weather forecasts, sports, and entertainment. The age of **cinema** blossomed thanks to electricity.

Ovens, washing machines, refrigerators, irons, and other appliances were powered by electricity. Light and heat gave families more time together in the evening.

STILL IN THE DARK

Many places around the world have little to no access to electricity. About 1.1 billion people do not have electricity at all. People who live in areas far from cities might only have electricity a few hours a day or less.

Early refrigerators looked very different from modern ones. They stored much less food and had very small freezer sections.

THE FUTURE OF ELECTRICITY

Human innovation brought electricity to the world. But electricity comes at a cost. Most power plants in the United States burn coal or gas to produce the movement that is used to generate electricity. These plants produce **greenhouse gases** that are harmful for the environment. Water, wind, and solar energy offer alternative energy sources for electricity that cause less pollution.

Solar panels harness energy from sunlight.

But making the change to new power sources is not easy. It is expensive and controversial. Meanwhile, many people are working to conserve the energy they have. Conservation saves money and helps the environment, and there are lots of choices you can make to help reduce greenhouse gases.

What can we do to conserve electricity at home?

- Use light-emitting diode (LED) light bulbs, which use less electricity and last much longer than incandescent bulbs.

- Replace furnaces and air conditioning units with heat pumps.

- Include a lot of insulation and energy-saving windows if you are building a new house.

- Use energy-efficient kitchen and laundry appliances instead of older ones.

Most of the world depends on electricity to live and work. The ability to harness electricity remains one of the greatest discoveries in history. Innovators continue to explore new ways to produce and conserve this amazing invention that changed the world.

GLOSSARY

cinema (SIN-uh-muh): the movie and film industry

convert (kuhn-VURT): change into something else

currents (KUR-uhnts): flows of electric charge

electrons (ih-LEK-trahns): small charged particles, part of the atoms that make up matter, whose movement results in electricity

greenhouse gases (GREEN-hous GAS-ehz): gases such as carbon dioxide and methane that collect in the atmosphere, prevent the sun's heat from escaping, and result in Earth's warming

hydraulic (hye-DRAW-lik): powered by liquid being forced under pressure through pipes

incandescent (in-kuhn-DES-uhnt): glowing with intense light and heat

innovations (in-uh-VAY-shuhns): new ideas or inventions

transmitted (trans-MIH-ted): sent or passed something from one place to another

voltage (VOHL-tij): the force of an electrical current, expressed in volts

INDEX

TEXT-DEPENDENT QUESTIONS

1. What are three power sources that create less greenhouse gas?
2. How was food kept fresh before electricity?
3. Who opened the first U.S. central power plant?
4. What are three ways that electricity changed households?
5. How can you improve a house to conserve electricity?

EXTENSION ACTIVITY

Pick an electrical appliance in your home that is used for a chore. Try doing the chore without that appliance. Was it more or less work? Write about how doing the chore with and without the appliance was different.

ABOUT THE AUTHOR

Robin Koontz loves to learn and write about everything from abalone to ziggurats. Raised in Maryland and Alabama, Robin now lives with her husband in the Coast Range of western Oregon. She especially enjoys observing the diverse wildlife on her property. You can learn more on her blog at robinkoontz.wordpress.com.

www.rourkeeducationalmedia.com

PHOTO CREDIT: Cover: ©heibaihui, ©Cappan; page 5: ©Beyhes Evren; pages 6-7, 15c, 20-21, 21b, 22-23: ©LOC; page 8: ©David_ Johnson; page 9: ©Skyhobo; page 10: ©Food_drive; page 11: ©fergregory; page 12a: ©Morphart Creation; page 12b: ©newscom; page 13: ©thepropshoppe; pages 14-15: ©Cappan; page 15a: ©Andrew Linscolt; page 15b: ©Silberkorn; pages 16-17: ©Museum of Innovation and Science Schenectady via GE; pages 18-19: ©akg-images; page 21a: ©wiki; page 24: ©KarenHBlack; page 25: ©Everett Historical; pages 26-27: ©Shvv; page 28: ©Trigem777; page 28-29: ©gerenme

Edited by: Tracie Santos
Cover and interior layout by: Kathy Walsh

Library of Congress PCN Data

Invention of Electricity / Robin Koontz
(It Changed the World)
ISBN 978-1-73162-983-8 (hard cover)(alk. paper)
ISBN 978-1-73162-976-0 (soft cover)
ISBN 978-1-73162-989-0 (e-Book)
ISBN 978-1-73163-335-4 (ePub)
Library of Congress Control Number: 2019945573

Rourke Educational Media
Printed in the United States of America,
North Mankato, Minnesota